Careers in Nanomedicine

Martin Gitlin

Published in the United States of America by
Cherry Lake Publishing, Ann Arbor, Michigan
www.cherrylakepublishing.com

Reading Adviser: Marla Conn, MS, Ed., Literacy specialist, Read-Ability, Inc.

Photo Credits: Cover, anyaivanova; page 4 (left), eHrach; Page 4 (right), Riksa Prayogi; page 6, Moreno Soppelsa; page 8, science photo; page 10, Gorodenkoff; page 12, Diego Cervo; page 14 Syda Productions; page 16, anyaivanova; page 18, HaHanna; page 20, Oleg Mikhaylov; page 22, Volodymyr Horbovyy; page 24, Tyler Olson; page 26, angellodeco; page 28, Shawn Hempel. Source: Shutterstock.

Library of Congress Cataloging-in-Publication Data

CIP data has been filed and is available at catalog.loc.gov.

Printed in the United States of America.

Table of Contents

Hello, Emerging Tech Careers!

In the past ...

Groundbreaking inventions made life easier in many ways.

In the present ...

New technologies are changing the world in mind-boggling ways.

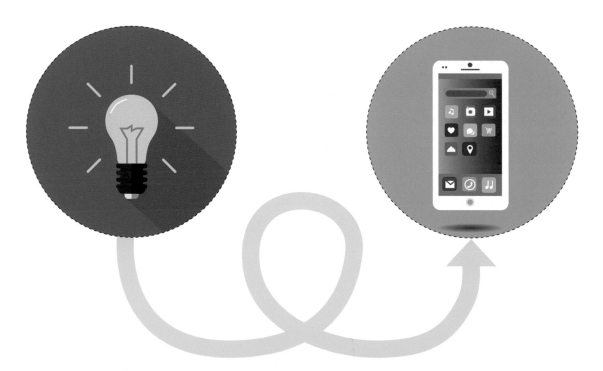

The future is yours to imagine!

WHAT COMES NEXT?

Who would have thought?

Alexander Graham Bell invented the first telephone in 1876. In 1879, Thomas Edison invented the first electric lightbulb. The Wright brothers successfully flew the first airplane in 1903. And don't forget Henry Ford! He invented a way to make cars quicker and cheaper.

These brilliant inventors did things that people once thought were impossible. To go from candles to electricity? From horse-drawn carriages to automobiles and airplanes? Wow!

The sky's the limit!

Now technology is being used to do even more amazing things! Take **nanomedicine**, for instance. Nanomedicine involves engineering teeny tiny machines to prevent and treat diseases in the human body. It can be used in endless ways—from treating cancer to providing needleless shots. Some day it may even be possible for nano-robots to perform surgery!

This book explores the people and professions behind nanomedicine. Some of these careers, like nanotechologist, are so cutting-edge that they didn't exist just a decade or so ago. Others, like chemist, offer exciting new twists using nanomedicine.

Read on to explore exciting possibilities for your future!

Biomedical Engineer

You make choices every day. Should I have cereal or toast for breakfast? Do I want to watch cartoons on TV or check out the Internet? Biomedical engineers get to make choices too. Some work in physical science. Others in computer science. Still others in **engineering**. But they can all help the world of nanomedicine.

Biomedical engineering is a very broad field. It uses the knowledge and talent of those working in many areas of engineering. It also makes use of chemistry, cell biology, **genetics**, veterinary medicine, and human medicine.

What do biomedical engineers use all that knowledge to do? They design products for the health care industry. They create equipment like artificial body parts and organs. They design machines for diagnosing medical problems and instruments that doctors use. They explore devices that control the rate in which medicines are given to people—for example, the injection of drugs that last a month or more in the body.

Another important job they have is developing new medicines. They look deeper at how human cells and tissues will be affected by them. They evaluate how effectively the medicines might treat patients before they are even used. And they assess the success or failure of medicines once they're in the body.

Imagine It!

➔ Remember the last time you or a family member had a cold or the flu?

➔ Make a list of the worst symptoms.

➔ Now, imagine that a nano-robot could have be added to your medicine. Describe in pictures or words what it could have done to help you feel better?

Dig Deeper!

✔ The following website states that cells are the "structure of life": https://kidsbiology. com/biology-basics/ cell-structure/.

✔ Look around the website. Then use what you learn to draw a picture of a human cell.

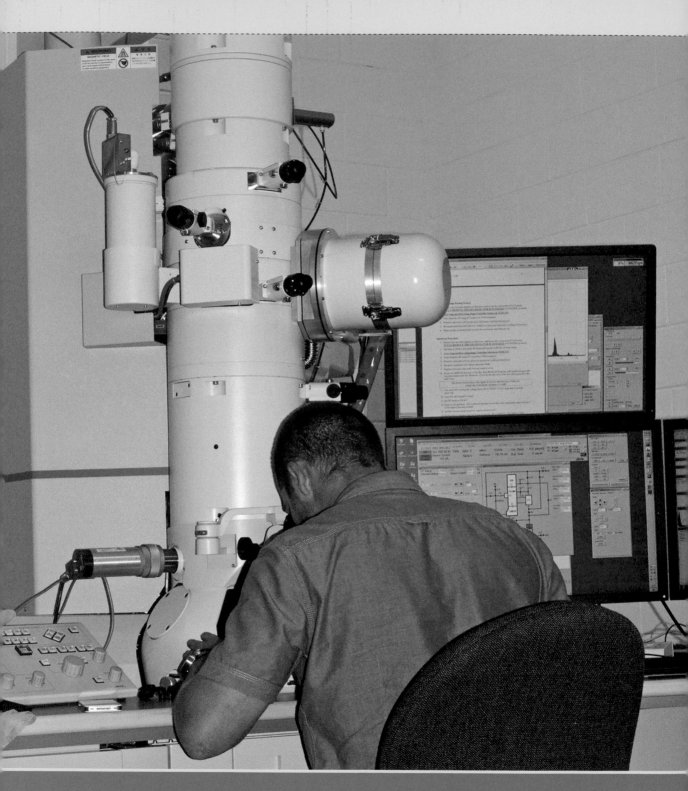

Biomedical engineers often use powerful microscopes.

Biomedical engineers work with artificial cells as well. These are small capsules that replace body cells. Some capsules are used to deliver drugs. But remember: This is all done on the tiniest, or nano, scale!

Biomedical engineers are not alone in their research. They work with other scientists. They might oversee a staff of biomedical equipment technicians. They spend most of their time in hospitals, universities, and laboratories.

Biomedical engineers create concepts and tools used in engineering, physical science, medicine, and life science. Their work will be critical to the future of nanomedicine. They ensure that drug treatments will be safe and effective. They give doctors and patients peace of mind. They will continue pushing forward into new frontiers of knowledge, helping to find cures to many diseases. And that will help transform and improve patient care.

Future Biomedical Engineer

Those who wish to pursue this career should try to take advanced placement math and science courses in high school. Included are calculus, chemistry, computer programming, and physics. Great experience can be gained by going to engineering camps in the summer. A college degree in biomedical engineering is often required to launch a career.

Chemist

Is it possible to control things on a nanoscale, a size that's measured in **nanometers**? After all, a nanometer is one-billionth of a meter! It is possible.

When it comes to nanomedicine. you know what they say: Good things come in small packages!

Chemists in the world of nanomedicine are explorers. They focus on drug discovery and advancement. They look to plants and other natural sources to find healing properties. Then they find ways to mimic nature by developing new **synthetic**, or human-made, drug compounds.

Some of the medicines they research and create will be strong enough to cure illness and prevent disease. Others will improve the ways in which drugs are made. It is possible that some of these discoveries could lead to lower costs for medicines that people need.

Chemists who work in nanomedicine share one goal: To produce drugs that can be delivered safely and effectively using **nanoparticles**. Nanoparticles can also send heat, light, or other substances through the body. They target cells stricken with diseases such as cancer. Delivery on the nanoscale reduces damage to healthy cells. It even allows for early detection of disease.

Imagine It!

➜ Water can exist as a solid, liquid, or gas.

➜ Make a chart showing the characteristics of each form.

Dig Deeper!

✔ Click on the following website: www. chem4kids.com.

✔ Read at least three pages. Make a list of three cool things you learned about chemistry.

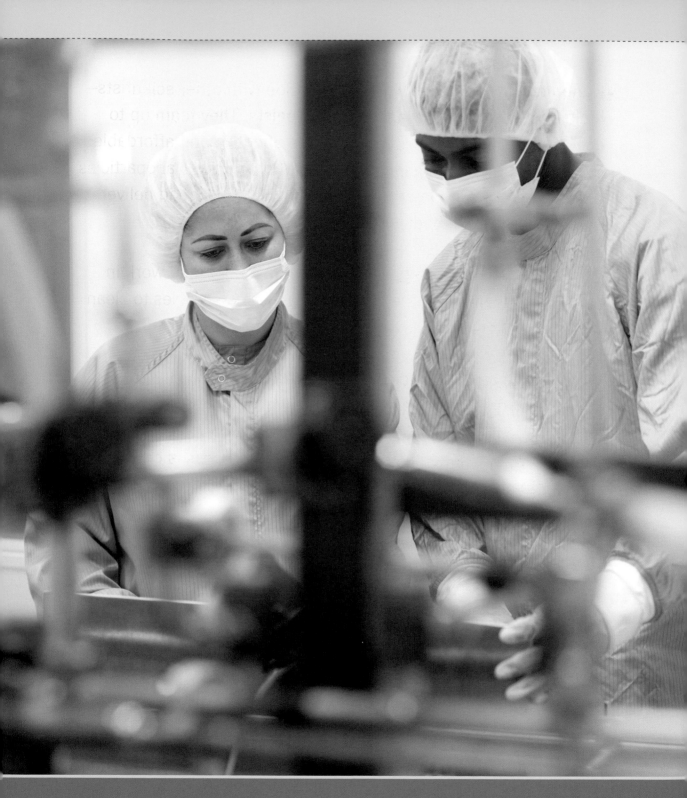

Some chemists work in super clean, or sterile, laboratories.

Nanomedicine chemists work side by side with other scientists—biologists, toxicologists, and microbiologists. They team up to develop and test new drugs that will be effective and affordable. Still, chemists are diving into new scientific territory. Nanoparticles remain in the development stage. Proving that they can deliver drugs in the human body will be a big step.

Not all **nanotechnology** chemists in the health field work in medicine. Others study the effects of nanoscale particles to clean polluted air or water. They also teach and train others.

Which drugs created by chemists will work? Which will not have the desired effect? Each drug goes through many rounds—and sometimes years—of testing. But it is certain that talented chemists will be needed in the future. Their success is critical for nanomedicine to reach the ultimate goals of curing illness and wiping out diseases.

Future Chemist

Several colleges and national laboratories offer research programs that focus on chemistry for nanotechnology. First, though, you should pursue a degree in chemistry or biology. That sets you on the path toward working as a chemist developing drugs for nanomedicine. Landing a good job generally requires an advanced degree and some research experience.

Molecular Biologist

They say that good things come in small packages. No one proves this true better than molecular biologists. They work to uncover big secrets hidden in tiny cells.

Molecular biologists are a natural fit for nanomedicine. Their science explores the structures and functions of cells on a molecular level. Nanomedicine treats cells on a molecular level. The research and findings of molecular biologists are critical to the success of nanomedicine. That makes this career promising and attractive.

Cell functions are complex and not easy to understand. This is true even when you are a molecular biologist! Interaction between molecules is what makes life possible. But there is still a lot to learn about how cells connect and cooperate with each other.

That is why they spend so much time researching the secrets of cells. In a way, their work is like that of a detective. They look for clues that help them solve mysteries about the ways cells work.

Their job is critical. They must gain more knowledge about the molecules that make up human cell tissue.

Imagine It!

→ Find out online how many cells are in the human body.

→ Write down your weight and your height in inches.

→ Use a calculator to figure out the average number of cells that are in your body per pound and per inch.

Dig Deeper!

✓ Read all about biology at the following website: https://kidsbiology.com/.

✓ What was the most eye-opening fact that you did not know before?

✓ Make a poster to share what you learned.

Molecular biologists use special tools to do their jobs.

Only then can they help nanomedicine battle diseases that strike those cells. The work of molecular biologists aids the entire process. Their discoveries help chemists design drugs that turn diseased cells into healthy ones. They help chemists create nanoparticles that deliver those drugs and other treatments into the body.

Molecular biologists toil in labs and universities. But not all of them work in the world of medicine. Some teach or share their knowledge with others. They explain what they do in terms that are easy to understand. Doctors are among those who have been trained by molecular biologists.

Nanomedicine is the wave of the future. The world of medicine depends on the new science in improving a wide range of treatments. And those who deliver that treatment will grow more reliant upon molecular biologists.

Future Molecular Biologist

One must secure a **PhD** in biochemistry, biology, physics, or a related field to work as a molecular biologist in research or development. You can earn a bachelor's or master's degree to gain an entry-level position in the field. But only those who further their education can advance.

Nanotechnologist

How do you work with something you can't see? Just ask a nanotechnologist. They help those working in many fields understand tiny particles called nanometers. This allows scientists and engineers to develop and advance amazing new products, some of which are used in the world of nanomedicine.

Look at a piece of paper. It's very thin, right? Well, that sheet of paper is 100,000 times thicker than the particles that nanotechnologists use. They work with particles that cannot even be seen with an ordinary telescope. Yet they transform those tiny particles into huge inventions.

A nanometer is about one-billionth of a meter. Particles on that scale cannot be touched with human hands. But nanotechnologists know how to make that size work for them. They create new materials one molecule at a time. That allows them to be precise while unlocking properties and power not otherwise available.

Nanotechnology delves into many sciences—physics, chemistry, biology, engineering, and computer science. They utilize research from those who work in all of these fields. They study and apply that information to nanoscale experiments. They seek to create new and improved products along the way.

Imagine It!

➔ Imagine you are the size of a nanoparticle. You are 100,000 times thinner than a piece of paper.

➔ Think of where you could go that you cannot go in your present size.

➔ Would you enjoy that? If so, for how long, before you yearned to return to human size?

Dig Deeper!

✔ *The Incredible Shrinking Man* is a 1957 science-fiction movie. It is about a man who shrinks down to nano size.

✔ Watch the end of the movie here at http://bit.ly/ShrinkMan.

✔ Write a story about how you would handle this situation if it happened to you.

Thanks to nanotechnology, sunscreens are now safer and more effective.

For instance, nanotechnologists have used their knowledge to improve sunscreen. The product has for years used zinc oxide and titanium dioxide to reflect sunlight that can cause cancer. The use of nanoparticles has improved it. Sunscreen can now safely absorb light and scatter visible light as well. Now it does not have to be applied as often. It is less likely to irritate skin or cause allergic reactions. And it is not as visible on human skin.

The science is still very new. But nanotechnologists are working to make a bigger impact on the medical field. They are developing nanoparticles that work like tiny **robots** to attack diseased cells in the human body. They are helping create new drugs and equipment. They are working to make sick people healthy.

Future Nanotechnologist

Those seeking a career as a nanotechnologist in the medical field should focus on math and science courses in high school. Either a medical degree or PhD, or both, are required. Other options in nanotechnology include agriculture and food scientist or electrical engineer. Both require a bachelor's degree.

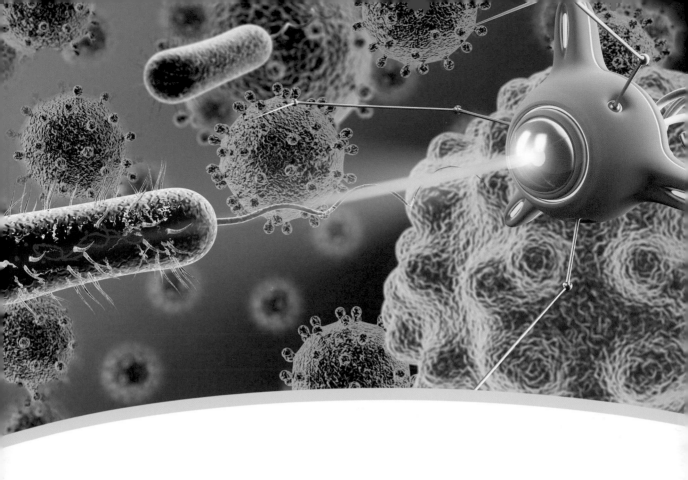

Physician

Doctors have one of the most important jobs in the world. They make sick people well. They can turn despair into joy. They can be a friend to someone who needs one. They can give hope to a person who feels hopeless. Their jobs can be hard and hectic. But they can save lives. Their careers can be very rewarding.

The role of doctors has expanded over time, and they have become more specialized. The testing and research of others have helped them become better in their work. As medicine becomes more advanced, so do they. Nanomedicine promises them a huge leap forward.

Doctors specialize in many different areas. Pediatricians treat children. Geriatric physicians work with old people. Some doctors handle problems common to men. Others deal with physical issues of women.

Physicians also focus on specific body parts. Podiatrists work on feet. Ear, nose, and throat doctors treat those body parts. Ophthalmologists help folks see better. Cardiologists treat the heart. Dermatologists are skin doctors. Rheumatologists diagnose and cure diseases of the joints.

Some specialists might benefit more than others from the growth of nanomedicine. But treating people through new and advanced methods should aid doctors in a wide range of specialties.

Imagine It!

➡ List as many body parts that come to mind.

➡ Find a list online of different kinds of doctors.

➡ Make a chart to match the correct doctors with the body parts they treat.

Dig Deeper!

✔ The following website teaches first aid to kids: http://bit.ly/FirstAidKids.

✔ Make a list of 10 tips you can use in case of emergencies.

Nanomedicine often provides doctors with better options for treating very sick patients.

Nanomedicine could also prove very helpful to those who perform operations. Surgeons seek methods that are less invasive to their patients. Minimally **invasive** surgeries mean less scarring and fewer post-surgery problems. The potential of nanotechnology is great for surgeons. Most intriguing is the potential of "nanobots." These are robots that could be shrunk for entry into the body through cavities. A nanobot controlled by surgeons using a computer could perform precise surgery within cells.

That cannot be done by humans. Surgical tools are simply too large. Scalpels are thousands of times bigger than a single cell.

Physicians do not create the various tools of nanomedicine. But they benefit from them. And they will gain more from nanomedicine as it grows. Physicians can look to their futures with optimism and excitement. Nanomedicine will make their jobs easier. It will help them treat illnesses and diseases far more effectively. And that has always been their goal.

Future Physician

Strong grades in math and science are necessary to becoming a doctor. High school students should excel in biology, physics, chemistry, and calculus. College students must perform well in premed classes before taking the Medical College of Admission Test. Next is four years of medical school, where more is learned about the human body, diseases, and treatment. The last step is at least three years of residency training before a medical license can be granted.

Research Scientist

Research scientists are curious people. They explore many options until they learn which is the best. This is certainly true with medical research scientists. They research and test and experiment to find ways to make sick people healthy.

What will make nanomedicine most effective in drug delivery? Or in medical therapy? Or in disease detection? Or in curing illness? Or in cell repair? You name it and research scientists search for solutions. They are the problem solvers of all sciences, and that includes nanomedicine. Research scientists explore everything in nanoscale that can make a difference.

Researchers have conducted many tests with nanoparticles that deliver drugs, heat, or light to diseased cells. For instance, they have tested a delivery method on mice that seeks better ways to send therapy drugs to cancer cells. The system uses gelatin to carry nanoparticles into the cell, where they dissolve.

Research scientists have studied nanoparticles that release drugs when struck by force. This is what happens when a drug hits a clotted artery. The system uses gelatin to carry nanoparticles directly into a diseased cell where the medicine starts its healing work.

Imagine It!

→ Imagine you can shrink down and travel through the human body.

→ Where would you want to go?

→ Draw pictures of your routes to the heart and brain.

Dig Deeper!

✓ Click on the following website: http://kidshealth.org/en/kids/htbw.

✓ Draw an outline of a human body.

✓ Using information you discover online, see how many systems and organs you can add to the picture.

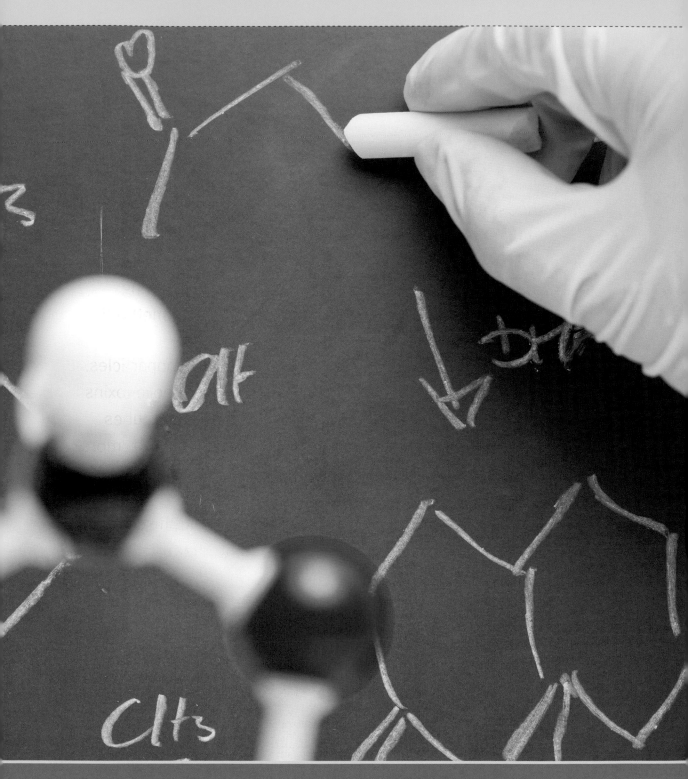

Every molecule matters when it comes to nanomedicine.

They have tested nanoparticles that can better deliver drugs to damaged brain tissue. They have even researched nanoparticles filled with radiation for treating cancerous tumors. That would allow more radiation safely into the body.

The methods of delivery tested by researchers vary. They have studied nanoparticles that can be taken by mouth. The particles would deliver drugs through the lining of the intestines and into the bloodstream. Patients would probably prefer swallowing a pill to getting a painful shot, which is also a delivery method!

Researchers have also worked outside the realm of nanoparticles. They have developed nanosponges that absorb and remove toxins (poisons) from the bloodstream. They have studied nanotubes that convert laser light to sound waves. These blast away tumors or other diseased areas without damaging healthy tissue.

Where there is a problem, there is a solution. Research scientists are working hard to find problems and eliminate them.

Future Research Scientist

Plan on a long college journey if you wish to pursue this career. Research scientists must major in biological science or medicine. A master's degree is required, but you still might not get hired without a PhD.

Can You Imagine?

Innovation always starts with an idea. This was true for Alexander Graham Bell, Thomas Edison, Henry Ford, and the Wright brothers. It is still true today as innovators imagine new ways to develo nanomedicine. And it will still be true in the future when you begin your high-tech career. So ...

What is your big idea?

Think of a cool way to use nanomedicine. Write a story or draw a picture to share your idea with others.

Glossary

engineering (en-juh-NEER-ing) the process of designing and building machines or structures

genetics (juh-NET-iks) the study of how personal characteristics are passed from one generation to another through genes

invasive (in-VAY-siv) involving entry into the body by cutting or by inserting medical instruments

nanomedicine (NAN-oh-med-ih-sin) the use of nanotechnology to prevent and treat diseases in the human body

nanometers (NAN-uh-mee-turz) units of measurement that are one-billionth of a meter; commonly used in nanotechnology in the building of extremely tiny machines

nanoparticles (NAN-uh-par-tih-kuhlz) small objects that behave as a whole unit with respect to their transport and properties; used in nanotechnology

nanotechnology (nan-oh-tek-NAH-luh-jee) the science of manipulating materials on an atomic or molecular scale, especially to build microscopic devices such as robots or medicine delivery

PhD (PEE AYCH DEE) the highest college degree, awarded to a person who has done advanced research in a particular subject; also called a doctorate

robots (ROH-bahts) machines that are programmed to perform complex human tasks

synthetic (sin-THET-ik) manufactured or artificial rather than found in nature

Index

About the Author

Martin Gitlin is a freelance author based in Cleveland. He has had more than 110 books published. He won more than 45 writing awards during his 11 years as a newspaper journalist, including first place for general excellence from the Associated Press. That organization selected him as one of the top four feature writers in Ohio in 2001.